KYOTO

THE CITY AT A GLAN

Kyoto Station

This huge, horizontally articula
designed by Hiroshi Hara, ope
It features a spectacular atriu
specially commissioned artwo.
See p010

Kyoto Tower

Erected in 1964 to attract tourist yen away
from the Tokyo Summer Olympics, Mamoru
Yamada's controversial 131m tower has an
observation deck with fantastic panoramas.
See p009

Higashi Honganji

The original 1602 temple here was destroyed
in a fire. The current structure, which is one
of the largest timber-framed buildings in the
world, dates from 1895.
*Karasuma-dori, Shichijo-agaru,
Shimogyo-ku, T 075 371 9181*

Nishi Honganji

The Goeido and Amidado halls that comprise
this ornate UNESCO World Heritage-listed
complex were constructed in 1636 and 1760.
*Horikawa-dori, Hanayacho-sagaru,
Shimogyo-ku, T 075 371 5181*

Kiyomizudera

Head up through Higashiyama to the 'Pure
Water Temple' for superlative views, and to
drink from one of the springs, said to either
prolong life, sharpen the mind or help find
love. Sampling all three is considered greedy.
See p014

Arashiyama

'Stormy Mountain' is totally unspoilt. Take in
the wooden Togetsukyo bridge, and explore
the bamboo groves and Tenryuji temple.
See p033

INTRODUCTION
THE CHANGING FACE OF THE URBAN SCENE

It might be only the country's seventh largest city by population yet Kyoto punches well above its weight due to the millennium it spent as Japan's seat of power. Its cultural heritage is astonishing, from temples to shrines, gardens and *machiya* (wooden houses) – still standing thanks to a merciful lack of earthquakes and a decision by the US not to bomb it in WWII. But this is no timeworn relic living off its legacy. Since the samurai battles of the 15th century, Kyoto has avoided confrontation by preserving the old and tolerating the new, which is what makes it so alluring. In the 1960s, Kyotoites came to accept that things had to change if their hometown were to remain dynamic, and today the city that brought the world the classical theatre forms *noh* and *kabuki* is just as famous for being the birthplace of Kyocera and Nintendo, and the location of the signing of the 1997 Kyoto Protocol treaty on climate change.

Visitors still come for the old landmarks, but what they find is a place where mixologists use tea-ceremony techniques to pour a single malt in a bar that is so minimal you cannot see any bottles; where 100-year-old architecture is no longer razed but repurposed for 21st-century retail and leisure; and where artisans use ancestral methods to make fabric for Lady Gaga's shoes. Soak up its ancient history, but also witness the modernity that introduced us to two pixelated Italian plumbers called the Super Mario Brothers. The former capital is as vibrant and creative as it ever was.

ESSENTIAL INFO
FACTS, FIGURES AND USEFUL ADDRESSES

TOURIST OFFICE
Kyoto Tourist Information
2nd floor, JR Kyoto Station Building
Shimogyo-ku
T 075 343 0548

TRANSPORT
Airport transfer to city centre
The Kansai-Airport Express Haruka to
Kyoto Station takes 80 minutes
www.hyperdia.com
Public transport
Trains run from 5.30am to midnight
www.city.kyoto.lg.jp/kotsu
Taxis
MK Taxi
T 075 778 4145
It's safe and easy to hail cabs on the street

EMERGENCY SERVICES
Ambulance/Fire
T 119
Police
T 110
Late-night pharmacy
Sakura Pharmacy
841-2 Higashi Shiokoji-cho,
Shiokoji-dori, Shimogyo-ku
T 075 353 2066

CONSULATES
British Consulate-General
19th floor, Epson Osaka Building
3-5-1 Bakuro-machi, Chuo-ku
Osaka
T 066 120 5600
www.ukinjapan.fco.gov.uk
US Consulate-General
2-11-5 Nishitenma, Kita-ku
Osaka
T 066 315 5900
osaka.usconsulate.gov

POSTAL SERVICES
Post office
843-12 Higashi Shiokoji-cho, Shimogyo-ku
T 057 094 3790
Shipping
UPS
T 035 484 5834

BOOKS
Geisha of Gion by Mineko Iwasaki
(Pocket Books)
Houses and Gardens of Kyoto
by Thomas Daniell (Tuttle Shokai)
**Kyoto: An Urban History of Japan's
Premodern Capital** by Matthew Stravos
(University of Hawaii Press)
The Temple of the Golden Pavilion
by Yukio Mishima (Vintage Classics)

WEBSITES
Art
www.kyotocity-kyocera.museum
Newspaper
www.japantimes.co.jp

EVENTS
Kyoto Experiment
www.kyoto-ex.jp
Kyotographie
www.kyotographie.jp

COST OF LIVING
Taxi from Kansai Airport to city centre
¥35,000
Cappuccino
¥550
Packet of cigarettes
¥450
Daily newspaper
¥230
Bottle of champagne
¥7,000

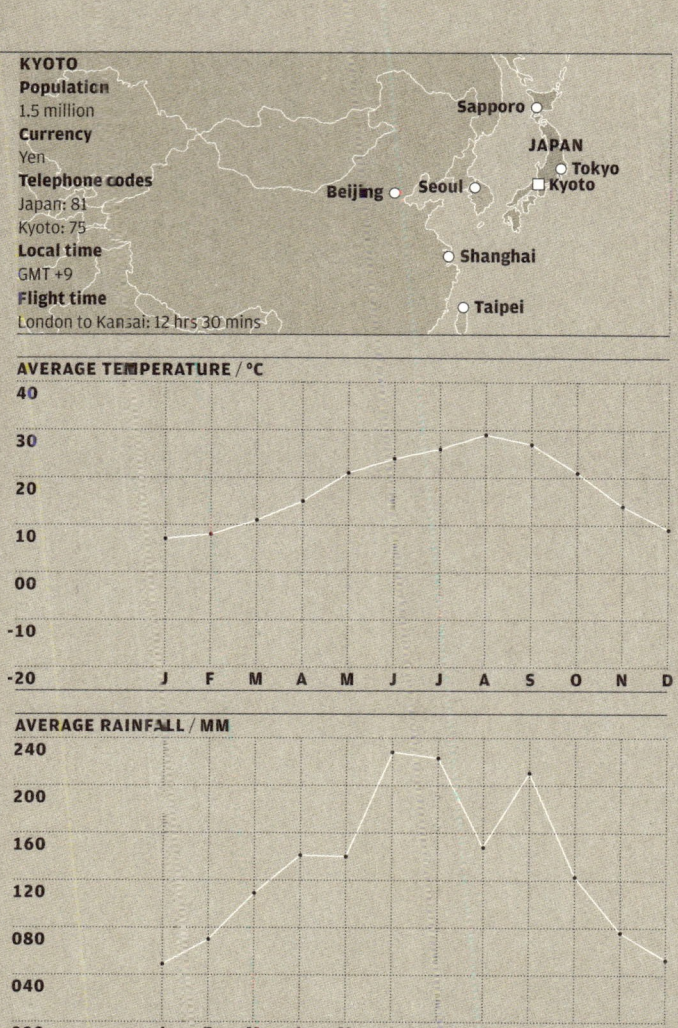

KYOTO

Population
1.5 million

Currency
Yen

Telephone codes
Japan: 81
Kyoto: 75

Local time
GMT +9

Flight time
London to Kansai: 12 hrs 30 mins

Sapporo

JAPAN

Tokyo

Beijing Seoul Kyoto

Shanghai

Taipei

AVERAGE TEMPERATURE / °C

	J	F	M	A	M	J	J	A	S	O	N	D

40
30
20
10
00
-10
-20

AVERAGE RAINFALL / MM

240
200
160
120
080
040
000

| J | F | M | A | M | J | J | A | S | O | N | D |

NEIGHBOURHOODS

THE AREAS YOU NEED TO KNOW AND WHY

To help you navigate the city, we've chosen the most interesting districts (see below and the map inside the back cover) and colour-coded our featured venues, according to their location; those venues that are outside these areas are not coloured.

ARASHIYAMA

This area offers pristine mountain forests and a picturesque landscape that changes spectacularly with the seasons. A scenic train meanders through idyllic Hozukyo valley (see p033) and tourist boats ply the Hozugawa river, cruising from Kameoka to Arashiyama. Nestled in the foothills is the serene 14th-century temple Tenryuji (68 Susukinobaba-cho, T 075 881 1235), set in a garden conceived by the Zen master and landscape artist Muso Soseki.

KINKAKUJI

Head to this district to visit Ryoanji (see p034), with its beguiling stone and sand garden, the World Heritage-listed temples Ninnaji (33 Omuro-dairi, T 075 461 1155) and Kinkakuji (see p013), and the joyous Insho-Domoto Museum of Fine Arts (26-3 Kamiyanagi-cho, T 075 463 0007), which was designed by the painter Insho Domoto to display his own works. Use the Keifuku Kitano line trams to explore the area.

GINKAKUJI

For an insight into Japanese architecture, take a trip to Ginkakuji (2 Ginkakuji-cho, T 075 771 5725). The shrine for the 15th-century shogun Ashikaga Yoshimasa is one of the most refined structures of the era, yet it is the smaller Togudo building that most influenced the vernacular, from private homes to the teahouse. Ginkakuji marks the start of Tetsugaku-no-michi, the bloom-laden Philosopher's Path.

OKAZAKI

Here you will find Kyoto's youngest major shrine, the 19th-century Heianjingu, and the Goichi Takeda-designed Prefectural Library (9 Seishoji-cho, T 075 762 4655). Check out the ancient Japanese art in the Hosomi Museum (6-3 Saishoji-cho, T 075 752 5555), that of the past century at the National Museum of Modern Art (see p068), where a reading room overlooks Japan's tallest torii (see p012), and the contemporary wing at Kyocera (see p036).

KARASUMA/KAWARAMACHI

These two inner areas, linked by Shijo-dori, are shopping heaven. Boutiques, cafés and galleries line the lanes. Browse the outlets within the Fumitsubaki Building (79 Mikura-cho, Sanjo-dori, Karasuma Nishi-iru), the upmarket department store Fujii Daimaru (605 Teinanmaeno-cho, Shijo-sagaru, Teramachi-dori, T 075 221 8181) and the retail hub Cocon Karasuma (620 Suiginya-cho, Karasuma-dori, T 075 352 3800).

GION/HIGASHIYAMA

If you are looking for old Kyoto, it is all here: the Buddhist temple Kiyomizudera (see p014), photogenic Shinto shrines, such as Yasaka-jinja (625 Gionmachi Kitagawa, T 075 561 6155), cobblestones, *geiko* (the local term for geisha), rickshaws and the Kamogawa river. Gion also has plenty of chic shops, the Sfera Building (see p094) and some excellent restaurants including Kikunoi (see p040) and Tan (see p054).

LANDMARKS

THE SHAPE OF THE CITY SKYLINE

Traditionalists have long bemoaned the modernisation of Kyoto. In the 1950s, the decision to build the Mamoru Yamada-designed Kyoto Tower (721-1 Higashi Shiokoji-cho, Karasuma-dori, Shimogyo-ku, T 075 361 3215), the city's tallest structure, sparked protests, and almost four decades later, architect Hiroshi Hara admitted to doubts about proceeding with his large-scale masterplan for the main station (overleaf), so vociferous was the public outcry. But historic Kyoto has remained largely untouched. In Gion, where the old and the new intersect most strikingly, power lines have been buried so that the *machiya*-lined streets are not tainted by steel and concrete. And beautiful temples such as Kinkakuji (see p013), Kiyomizudera (see p014) and Ryoanji (see p034) still stand in centuries-old gardens ringed by ancient forests.

However, the city looks to the future as much as the past, and when you have had your fill of pretty shrines, the upscale shopping clusters of Kawaramachi and Shijo-dori will swiftly transport you back into the 21st century. Navigating the central districts is easy enough, but note that there is no formal street-numbering system, and a maze of lanes runs along the Kamogawa riverfront and its canals. Although the addresses here will get you close to the temple or tearoom you are seeking, it's advisable to ask your concierge or *nakai-san* (maid) at your ryokan to mark destinations on a map. *For full addresses, see Resources.*

Kyoto Station

One of the most striking architectural statements in Kyoto, the city's main station is surprisingly underexplored. Arriving after a long bullet-train ride, few people venture beyond its central hall (pictured); it's a shame, as Hiroshi Hara's futurist edifice has many hidden spaces, such as a theatre, museum and wide staircase leading to a roof garden.
Higashi Shiokoji-cho, Karasuma-dori

Heianjingu

Not all of Kyoto's most famous shrines are ancient. Heianjingu was built in 1895 (the construction was overseen by Japan's first historian of architecture, Chuta Ito), and marks the city's 1,100th anniversary. It was remodelled in 1940, then partly rebuilt again in 1979, after fire ravaged the main building. Everything about it is impressive. A 24m-high, bright-red concrete-and-steel torii (above) marks the entrance to the shrine, and about 800m away is the *outen-mon* (main gate), from where you get a first glimpse of Ito's main hall and the three-roofed 'Blue Dragon Tower'. The gardens, conceived by Meiji-era master landscaper Jihei Ogawa, are planted with cherry trees and some 2,000 irises, and are considered to be a national treasure.
97 Nishi Tenno-cho, T 075 761 0221,
www.heianjingu.or.jp

Kinkakuji

Visiting Kyoto without seeing this World Heritage site, also known as the Golden Pavilion, would be like going to Sydney and missing the Opera House. So forget that the 600-year-old original was burnt down in 1950 by a 21-year-old monk (a story told by Yukio Mishima in his novel *The Temple of the Golden Pavilion*), and marvel at the three-storey replacement built in 1955, and covered in around 50kg of gold leaf in 1987. The structure blends Zen, samurai and imperial styles, and is surrounded by the lotus-filled Kyoko-chi (Mirror Pond), which features a Buddhist stone arrangement. Its layout and that of the generous garden pay homage to the visionary Muso Soseki (see p070), who died in the mid 14th century but whose concepts still influence Japanese landscaping today.
1 Kinkakuji-cho, T 075 461 0013

Kiyomizudera

A temple has stood here since AD778, but it has been rebuilt several times due to fires. The main hall dates from the early 17th century. Built on a slope in the *kake-zukuri* (overhanging) style, it juts out over a precipice, supported by 139 precisely cut pillars. Its huge cypress-shingle roof is said to be broad enough to accommodate all the Buddhist faiths.
1-294 Kiyomizu, T 075 551 1234

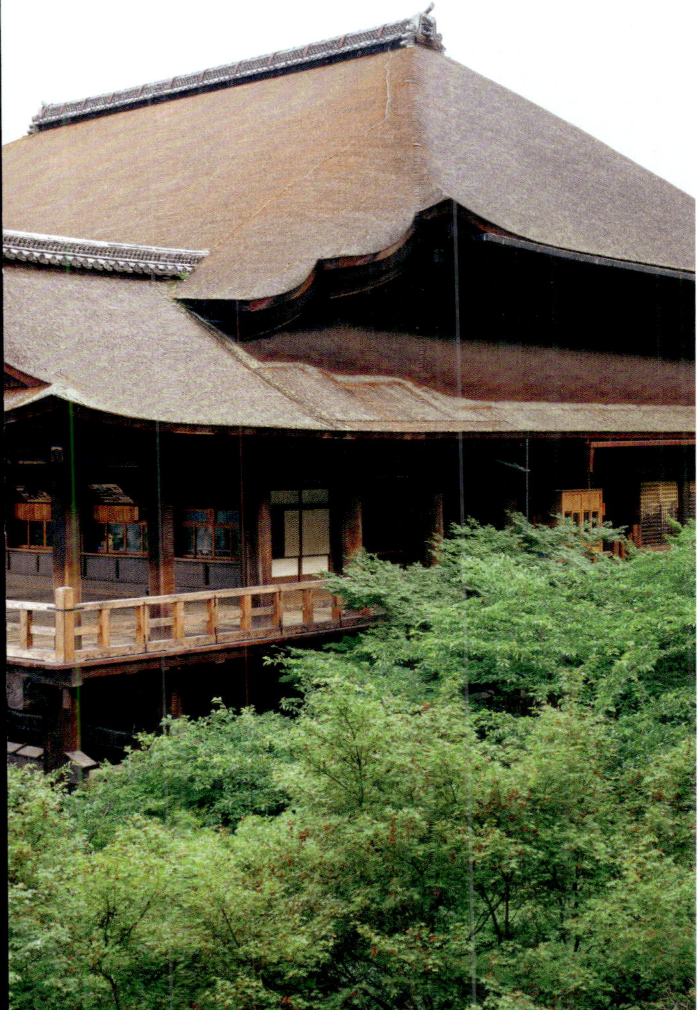

HOTELS

WHERE TO STAY AND WHICH ROOMS TO BOOK

Before you tell your white-gloved taxi driver which hotel you are staying at, pay attention to its name. In this city, which was once home to the Emperor and still boasts a royal guest house, monikers including The Royal Park Sanjo, Rihga Royal, Grand Prince and Hyatt Regency mean a right royal mix-up is easy to achieve.

Boutique hotels, some renovations of vernacular architecture, others focusing on alternative experiences, foster close encounters with local culture, and are often so discreet they pass for residences, such as The General (see p031) and the self-catering apartments at 22 Pieces (9-4 Higashikujo Muromachi, Minami-ku, T 075 644 5115), which offers guests 22 Japanese objects to borrow, while the ryokan Sowaka (480 Kiyoi-cho, Yasaka Toriimae-sagaru, T 075 541 5323) is a Taisho-era *ryotei* redesigned by Shigenori Uoya.

Headline global arrivals have been the Four Seasons (see p030) and, in 2020, Ace (245-2 Kurumaya-cho), Kengo Kuma's reworking of Tetsuro Yoshida's 1926 Central Telephone Office with a latticed timber facade, verdant garden courtyard and bespoke interiors by Commune Design. Budget digs have impressive design credentials too, from Maja (92 Tsuchiya-cho, Yanaginobamba-dori, T 075 205 5477), a Nordic take on the capsule hotel replete with swathes of wood and Marimekko textiles, to 9h (see p018) and chic art hostel Kumagusuku (37-3 Mibubamba-cho, Nakagyo-ku, T 075 432 8168). *For full addresses and room rates, see Resources.*

Hotel Kanra

Architect Norito Nakahara converted this five-storey 1980s cram school near Higashi Honganji (see p077) in 2010 and then more than doubled its size six years later, and it retains an educational remit in its aim to inform guests about Kyoto culture. The 68 long rooms are inspired by the layout of a *machiya*, with volcanic stone floors, raised tatami-mat seating areas, swathes of pale wood, and Q nude skincare products made from silk by local kimono firm Chiso; the Kanra Suite (above) has a fragrant cypress tub on its balcony garden. There are DIY kits and classes on the likes of calligraphy and ikebana, and the signature of teppanyaki restaurant Hanaroku (T 075 344 3829) is Wagyu beef, and small-batch artisan sake. *190 Kitamachi, Karasuma-dori, Rokujo-sagaru, Shimogyo-ku, T 075 344 3815, www.hotelkanra.jp*

9h

Spending the night in a capsule hotel is a rite of passage for Japanese workers who have missed the last train home, but until 9h arrived, the experience had never been this chic. Designed by Fumie Shibata and Takaaki Nakamura, a hive-like layout of white sleeping pods (50 for women, 75 for men, on separate floors) is set in a black wall. Opened in 2009, 9h is popular with travellers thanks to its central location, affordability and easy-to-read pictograms by graphic artist Masaaki Hiromura. On the third and ninth floors there is lock-up storage. Check in, have a relaxing shower, then crawl into your tube. A light acts as an alarm clock, slowly brightening until you awake, without disturbing the neighbours.
588 Teianmaeno-cho, Teramachi-dori, Shijo-sagaru, T 075 353 7337, www.ninehours.co.jp/kyoto

RC Hotel

To stay in a modern structure in historic Higashiyama may be counterintuitive, but RC Hotel has its own retro charm. A small mult-storey apartment block built in the 1970s before height restrictions prevented further urbanisation of the area, it retains many brutalist elements, including exterior corridors, weathered metal doors and an open roof, from where there's a stunning view of Yasaka Pagoda and the surrounds.

Inside, the raw concrete shell is textured with white paint and offset by the warm tones of midcentury-style wood furniture and pristine tiled bathrooms. The floors are themed as Vegetation, Folk Handicraft and Art (Room 302, above), which features exhibitions by emerging talents. The cosy bar serves Kyoto beers and sake.
370 Yasaka Kamimachi, T 075 354 5406, www.rchotelkyoto.com

Shiki Juraku

A renovation of a near-century-old enclave of terraced *machiya* in a residential district close to the Imperial Palace, Shiki Juraku is secreted behind a Tsuyoshi Tane bronze gate. The 10 individual two-storey dwellings have open beamwork, hinoki, ceramic or stone baths and vintage-inspired furniture, complemented by ikebana, bamboo pieces and abstract photos by Taisuke Koyama. The washi-covered walls are an exquisite feature in the main bedroom (above) of Ichi-go No 1 (opposite). The breakfast is a delight of farm-fresh salad, eggs, local bread and organic fruit juice served in an intimate salon; its sumptuous crimson walls, floorboards and bar seem to glow in natural light from the courtyard garden. *165 Konoe-cho, Shimodachiuri-agaru, Aburanokoji-dori, Kamigyo-ku, T 075 417 0210, www.shikijuraku.com*

Hiiragiya

Established as a ryokan in 1818, Hiiragiya, or 'House of the Holly Trees', has been run by the same family since its inception. In keeping with tradition, water is sprinkled over the stone floor at the entrance (above) to welcome guests. Inside, carp flicker in a pond, *saga* masks decorate the walls and water is drawn in *kouyamaki* (aromatic pine) baths to the perfect temperature; the *oke* (wooden buckets) and stools, used to wash before entering the tub, are crafted by Kiyotsugu Nakagawa and his son Shuji. It's not surprising that international film stars and Japan's royal family head here for solitude. Reserve a Tokubetsu-shitsu room, or spend a night in the Jun Michida-designed extension, completed in 2006. *Nakahakusan-cho, Fuyacho-dori, Aneyakoji-agaru, T 075 221 1136, www.hiiragiya.co.jp*

Node Hotel

A marriage of architectural minimalism by Seiichiro Takeuchi and bespoke interiors by Daisuke Enomoto of furniture company Indian Creek Fete, Node models itself on an art collector's home – and the works here are stellar. Its 25 rooms showcase original pieces by the likes of Tomoo Gokita, Shinro Ohtake and Yukimasa Ida against gentle grey interiors, from plush bedspreads and custom-made lamps to monotone walls and exposed-concrete ceilings. In the darkened hallways, spot-lit alcoves display further photographs, paintings and ceramics. The ground floor (lobby, above) is a convivial space, encompassing a lounge, a bar and a café/restaurant, that hosts larger works, a cabinet of sculptures and art books neatly laid out on a series of wooden tables.
461 Toroyama-cho, T 075 221 8800,
www.nodehotel.com

BnA Alter Museum

The gleaming pool of liquid that seems to seep from beneath the walls into the lobby/bar area is nothing to be alarmed about: it's art. It is also an indication of surprising things to come. This purpose-built 10-storey hotel's 31 unique rooms were designed by 16 Japanese creatives. From the intellectually conceptual to the borderline kitsch, each is an immersive installation. Bed down to Daito Manabe's audiovisual cloudscapes or Mizuguchi Guchi's nostalgic homage to Showa-era decor. The common areas including the café (pictured) host rotating exhibitions and there are regular events in the bar. Even the fire escape stairwell functions as a self-titled museum — four vitrine galleries host shows open to the public. *267-1 Tenma-cho, T 075 748 1278, www.bnaaltermuseum.com*

Hotel Anteroom

For decades, Kyoto's flat, industrial inner-city south was ignored, but the affordable rents, empty warehouses and accessibility are luring creative firms. The first name on the block was Anteroom. Occupying a 1980s student dorm revamped by Norito Nakahara and Koji Aoki in 2011, it doubled in size five years later. The lobby/gallery leads into a hip canteen area and lounge. Signage in a specially created typeface by Yuma Harada directs you to the 128 rooms, many of which retain their original (small) dimensions. The rates are very reasonable, so reserve an expansive Terrace Twin Room (204; above) with an outside patio, or one of the eight concept spaces by designers including Kohei Nawa and Mika Ninagawa. Most of the art on the walls is for sale.
7 Aketa-cho, Higashi-kujo, Minami-ku,
T 075 681 5656, hotel-anteroom.com

Hoshinoya

Arashiyama has been a resort ever since the 9th century, and Hoshinoya can trace its roots back 400 years. Architect Rie Azuma and landscaper Hiroki Hasegawa have created a 25-room hotel comprising a collection of luxury villas with chestnut floors, spruce-framed shoji screens and river views, two traditional gardens, and a sublime restaurant. Hoshinoya represents a modern refinement of classic Japanese design: the walls of each villa are lined with Kyoto-style *karakami* woodblock-printed paper by Takeo Honjo of Atelier Maruni; the pick is Tsukihashi (above). Surrounded by forest and overlooking the Ogawa, the super-secluded retreat is reached by boat – board at Togetsukyo ('Moon Crossing Bridge'; see p033). *11-2 Genrokuzan-cho, T 075 871 0001, www.hoshinoya.com*

Bijuu

Somewhat incongruously, Murakami-jyu, a heritage pickle merchant, launched this boutique property, housed in a five-storey building that was once a dowdy business hotel. The company approached Teruhiro Yanagihara to oversee the transformation; Room 501 (opposite) is the most spacious of the three individual suites, and is fitted with a private sauna and a huge stone tub in the living space (above). Room 301 is smaller, but has a kitchen and a *shikkui* (traditional plaster) wall. Each has bath products from local brand Aid, pottery by 1616 / Arita Japan and a Chemex coffee maker. Yanagihara also designed the chic second-floor restaurant Kiln (T 075 353 3555), which has a wood-fire oven at its heart and an interesting natural wine list. Alternatively, nearby Good Nature Station (see p052) has plenty of dining options.
194 Sendo-cho, Kiyamachi-dori, Shijo-sagaru, T 075 353 0802, www.bijuu.jp

Four Seasons

The Four Seasons is built around its star attraction, an 800-year-old *chisen kaiyu-shiki* (strolling garden). Its two ponds, tiny islands, rock arrangements, waterfall and pagoda are breathtaking in spring when more than 20 pink cherry-blossom trees bloom, and autumn when the maples turn fiery red. The rooms (Premier Garden View, above) are a celebration of contemporary artisanry – Nishijin fabric by Hosoo (see p066), *urushi* lacquerware, fusuma screens and Kaikado (see p095) caddies – and the spa treatments involve native ingredients, including a beautyberry facial. Overlooking the 12th-century landscaping, Fuju lounge serves local *wagashi* sweets, matcha tea, sake and champagne, and Brasserie fuses Japanese cuisine with French fine-dining.
445-3 Myohoin Maekawa-cho, T 075 541 8288, www.fourseasons.com/kyoto

The General

Kyoto's first dispersed hotel, The General's many properties, within walking distance of each other, are linked by Uchida Design Inc's warm minimalist interiors, and if you stay at one, you can use the facilities of all. The largest, Takatsuji Fuyacho, is the most luxurious and serene. Its 86 rooms embody Zen simplicity — pale wood furniture, white walls and monotone art. This aesthetic is softened in the cosy lounge, which faces an inner courtyard garden, by a palette of grey, olive and deep brown, gently lit in the evenings by *chochin*-style paper lanterns. The centrepiece here is an unusual portable tea-ceremony space with latticed bamboo panels and a raised floor (above). There is also a gym and a tatami-mat salon for yoga and workshops in crafts like *Kyo-karakami*. *241-1 Nabeya-cho, Takatsuji-agaru, Fuyacho-dori, T 075 746 3697, www.globalhotels.jp*

24 HOURS

SEE THE BEST OF THE CITY IN JUST ONE DAY

There's no escaping the fact that some of the best places to visit in Kyoto are packed with tourists, but some judicious scheduling will enable you to swerve the camera-carrying throng. The city is small enough, and its tram, bus and metro network reliable enough, to easily zip from one side to the other, yet our far-reaching itinerary here may still require a taxi or two – or rent a battery-powered bike from Kyoto Eco Trip (www.kyoto-option.com), who will drop off and collect from your hotel. If time is tight, stick to Gion, where you'll encounter iconic sights such as geisha click-clacking down the cobbles, teahouses and towering torii. You can also pack in a lot around Okazaki Park, home to a pair of landmark art museums (see p068), a beautiful brute of a cultural complex with a diverting café and bookstore (see p035) and many small galleries (see p065).

Much of Kyoto sleeps at a sensible hour, but a strip of venues by the canal off Kiyamachi-dori stay open until late. Nokishita711 (2-3-5 Sendo-cho, T 075 741 6564) is a bijou artisan gin bar with a nature-themed interior, and L'Escamoteur (138-9 Saito-cho, T 075 708 8511) is a cocktail den run by a French magician. A short stroll north, take the lift up to Cinematik Saloon (7F, 410 Shimomaruya-cho, T 075 251 0995), a hangout that's serious about its music and drinks. Nearby Urbanguild (Kiya-machi, Sanjo-sagaru, T 075 212 1125) is the city's most avant-garde space, hosting gigs, talk shows and abstract dance. *For full addresses, see Resources.*

09.00 Sagano Chikurin

Arashiyama, where the Oigawa becomes the Katsuragawa river, is the gateway to Kyoto's forested mountains. Walk through the bamboo groves of Sagano Chikurin in the morning mist from the Nonomiya-jinja shrine to Arashiyama Torroko station, then catch the retro Sagano Romantic Train. It snakes down a 7.3km track that threads its way along the river and over the Hozugawa bridge. The ride, which runs daily except certain Wednesdays (check online) from March to December, is not to be missed in autumn, when the trees take on a vibrant amber hue. If you have time, there is a 90-minute boat trip that departs from near the last stop, Kameoka Torokko station, and takes you back to Togetsukyo bridge. *Arashiyama Torokko station, Sagaogurayama Tabuchiyama-cho, T 075 861 7444, www.sagano-kanko.co.jp*

13.00 Ryoanji

The Muromachi-era (1336-1573) *karesansui-teien* (dry rock garden) at Ryoanji is one of the most contemplated in the world. In a 25m by 10m space surrounded by a clay wall, 15 stones are set out according to the golden ratio; only 14 can be seen at any one time, while the 15th, it is said, is visible only if the viewer has attained enlightenment. This 500-year-old World Heritage site is a magnet for architects, but all are drawn by its minimalist beauty. Just below the shrine, beside the Kyoyochi pond, is the Ryoanji Yudofuya restaurant (above), where top chefs serve exquisite *yudofu* (tofu hotpot) and other Buddhist *shojin-ryori* vegetarian dishes. Sitting at a low table, take in the lush landscaped scene outside, framed by the windows as if it were a painting.
13 Goryonoshita-machi, T 075 463 2216, www.ryoanji.jp

15.30 ROHM Theatre

High tea on the terrace of Kunio Maekawa's 1960 culture centre is a tranquil way to pass an afternoon. Sitting under the oversized concrete eaves that evoke the temples of Kyoto, you have a grandstand view of the sights of Okazaki Park (see p012). Inside the café/bar/restaurant, the soaring ceiling and windows lend the retro dining room a breeziness that is rare for this city. The modernist complex shows the influence of Maekawa's one-time teacher, Le Corbusier. It reopened in 2016 after a ¥11bn refit, overseen by Hisao Koyama, who updated the quake-proofing as well as the auditoria, which are used for opera and ballet. The upscale bookshop Tsutaya took space on the ground floor and stocks Kyoto's best selection of English-language titles. *13 Okazaki Saishoji-cho, T 075 771 6051, www.rohmtheatrekyoto.jp*

16.30 Kyocera Museum of Art

Inaugurated in 1933, this institution was designed by Kenjiro Maeda according to the Imperial Crown architectural style, with a copper roof and tiled facade. To bring it up to date in 2020, the city sold the naming rights to local firm Kyocera for 50 years to help pay for the renovation and extension. Architects Jun Aoki, the museum director, and Tezzo Nishizawa glazed over one of the courtyards (above) and added a 'glass ribbon' around the base and a new wing for contemporary art, which opened with a Hiroshi Sugimoto show. The permanent collection is strong in early 20th-century *nihonga*, featuring superlative pieces by Seiho Takeuchi and Shoen Uemura, and extends to current works including Miwa Yanagi's gender-critical photographic sets. *124 Okazaki Enshoji-cho, T 075 771 4334, www.kyotocity-kyocera.museum*

19.00 Namae no Nai Ramen

Jazz drifts from Bowers & Wilkins speakers, beer is served in Aritsugu aluminium cups, walls are gallery-white and the air is clean: 'No Name Ramen' is not your typical slurp joint. The counter is clutter-free. Napkins, chopsticks and condiments are stored in walnut drawers by carpenters Asakura Mokkou, who also made the elegant stools commissioned by owner Eitaro Yamada. Bubbling at the back (for 12 hours) is the 100-litre pot of tasty stock, ready to pour over noodles, pork, egg and vegetables. There is no sign – look for a filament bulb in front of a plain door, which leads to a concrete path through an indoor garden by landscaper Toshiya Ogino – and there's only about a dozen seats. But you should not have to wait long. Locals eat ramen fast, especially when it's this delicious.
534-31 Ebisu-cho, www.takakura-nijo.jp

22.00 Shuto Yanagino

There's minimalist. and then there's Shuto Yanagino. Owner Hironari Yanagino and architect Tetsu Kijima have conceived a space based on the concept of a *chashitsu* (tea ceremony room), installing a 6m-long counter formed from one piece of *bubinga* timber, and 10 chairs by local Naomi Toda. Affixed to the wall behind the bar is a vase that holds a single flower. There's no drinks list – that would be clutter – and instead Yanagino will listen to your preferences, suggest a cocktail and prepare it using graceful, practised movements. He also serves biodynamic wines and sakes by the glass. The wild garden is surprisingly big at 18m deep. The aesthetics and ritual are similar at alumnus Taichiro Ueda's Ueto Salon bar (T 075 751 5117) in Higashiyama.
33 Kamanza-cho, Sanjo-dori,
Shinmachi nishi-iru, T 075 253 4310

URBAN LIFE
CAFÉS, RESTAURANTS, BARS AND NIGHTCLUBS

The city is famous for its *kaiseki* and *Kyoto-ryori* cuisines, which combine *Kyo-yasai* – locally grown vegetables including *daikon* (radish) and *kujo negi* (green onion) – and high-quality tofu and *fu* (wheat gluten), a key Zen ingredient, to create complex dishes finely tuned to the seasons. There are more than 100 Michelin-star restaurants, serving all types of food from soba to sushi and *shojin-ryori*, the venerable meat-free diet of Buddhist monks. Locals are still split over whether Kitcho (see p056) is better than Kikunoi (459 Shimokawara-cho, Yasakatoriimae-sagaru, Shimokawara-dori, T 075 561 0015) or if, in fact, Hyotei (35 Kusagawa-cho, Nanzenji, T 075 771 4116) is superior. *Kaiseki* is pricey (and time-consuming); however, excellent cooking using quality produce can be enjoyed by every wage bracket – try Maker (see p048) and Tan (see p054).

As with the rest of Japan, the third-wave coffee boom is in full flow, seen at School Bus (see p044) and Walden Woods (see p058). For Kyoto-style tapas, squeeze into Yanagi Koji Taka (577 Nakano-cho, T 075 708 5791), a superb standing bar in a charming alleyway off Shijo-dori, and then go for craft beer at Takumiya (see p042) or gastropub Bungalow (15 Kashiwaya-cho, T 075 256 8205). Jazz fans should head to Greenwich House (577-5 Nakano-cho, Shinkyogoku-dori, Shijo-agaru, T 075 212 5041), a spot so delightfully intimate that the bar and band account for more than half of the floorplan.
For full addresses, see Resources.

Il Garage

Chefs Masato and Midori Shirakawa spent five years cooking in Italy before coming back to Kyoto and launching this elegant restaurant in 2018 in Midori's family home above a discrete garage, hence the name. Local firm Raku transformed it into a warm, inviting space in which the kitchen sits off to one side of an open room, and 'Elbow' chairs by Hans J Wegner match very nicely with the walnut tables and Bertrand Balas' 'Here Comes the Sun' pendants. The one small painting on the blue-grey walls is an heirloom. The menu reinterprets classic dishes with Japanese produce, for instance risotto with rock chives and Matsuba crab from Tottori. During hunting season, wild boar and venison often feature. The wine list centres around natural Italian varietals.

147 Doyu-cho, Sanjo-sagaru,
T 075 255 0936, www.ilgaragekyoto.com

Takumiya

Although Kyoto is inland from the Pacific and the Japan Sea, there is a distinctive maritime palette in the blue-and-white design of this craft beer bar, opened in 2015 by Takumi Shirashi, who previously lived on islands at either end the country, in Hokkaido and Okinawa. The line-up on tap changes regularly, but it's all sourced from Japan. Start with local heavyweights like Kyoto Brewing Co, Woodmill Brewery and Yamarido. The featherweight glasses are from Nakagawa Masashichi Shoten, and Shirashi commissioned his friends, such as ceramicist Makoto Nakata, for the tableware. Vibrant dishes might include steamed wild boar dumplings or a salad of asparagus and Manganji pepper with an umami-laden beetroot sauce.
400 Funaya-cho, Nakagyo-ku,
T 075 744 1675, www.takumiya.beer

Indépendants

This laidback spot is set in the basement of a beloved ferroconcrete building, designed in 1928 by Goichi Takeda and used as offices for a national newspaper. By 1998, it was facing demolition, but architect Hiroyuki Wakabayashi bought and restored it, with the help of local artists; Indépendants has retained parts of the original floor mosaics, while some of the lighting is by terrarium-maker Aki Murase. For two decades it has been a haunt of Kyoto's students, creatives and beret-wearers. The menu and wine list mostly draw from Spain (paella, tapas and sangria) but the bar also offers craft beers from Minoh (in Osaka) and a decent line-up of Japanese whisky. There are occasional free gigs. Upstairs, the Dohjidai Gallery of Art (T 075 256 6155) displays fresh talent.
1928 Building, 56 Benkeiishi-cho, Sanjo Gekomachi, T 075 255 4312

School Bus Coffee Stop

Parked in a converted car repair garage, School Bus is a slice of Americana, fitted out with retro and vintage furniture, close to the Imperial Palace. The café serves as a showcase for a parallel business, which is a design studio born in Osaka specialising in urban regeneration – Davada Coffee & Records (469-11 Zaimoku-cho), located in a previously disused building near Kyoto Station is one of its projects. The offering here is heavily influenced by global trends and delivered with Japanese hospitality. The standard coffee is a flat white, which is not a staple in Japan, and the baristas have a flair for latte art. Served until lunch, the French toast set is a mainstay; some days it's loaded with berries and fruit, on others it comes topped with a fried egg.
244 Daimonji-cho, Nakagyo-ku,
T 075 406 5002, www.schoolbus.coffee

Bar Rocking Chair

The name of this wood-bedecked cocktail bar does not disappoint. In fact, there are four rocking chairs, and they are the best seats in the house – pull one close to the open fire or to look out on to the interior garden. It is delightfully set in a *machiya*, down a cobblestone alley, furnished with antique heirlooms, including a century-old cabinet, while the counter is hewn from a single piece of walnut. Impeccably dressed owner Kenji Tsubokura won global acclaim in 2016 with his 'Best Scene' concoction, a mix of gin, elderflower liqueur, *yuzu*, lemon and cardamom bitters. The drinks offering is strong on port and national whiskies, and there's a menu of small plates such as Kyoto oil sardines and blue cheese thistle honey. *434-2 Tachibana-cho, Gokomachi-dori, Bukkoji-sagaru, T 075 496 8679, www.bar-rockingchair.jp*

Monk

For his *shime course*, the dish that ties up a meal, Yoshihiro Imai serves pizza (perhaps *kujo negi*, chrysanthemum or mackerel). It is a radical act when your cuisine is based on *kaiseki-ryori* but his take on the tradition is totally laden with surprises. He trained as a pizzaiolo at En Boca (T 075 253 0870) in Kyoto, and went on to write a seminal cookbook before setting up Monk in 2015. The design by Studio Doughnuts is simple, celebrating the view of the cherry blossom trees on the Philosopher's Path outside, and everything revolves around the oven, fired with *binchotan* and wood. The seven-part *omakase* menu depends on the ingredients sourced each morning in markets and small mountain farms. One signature is assorted grilled vegetables, with salt and olive oil.
147 Joodoji Shimominamida-cho,
T 075 748 1154, www.restaurant-monk.com

Maker

Chef Kei Yoshioka's 'borderless' concept
is executed via one communal table with
10 unassigned seats that fills the room,
which is decorated with dried herbs and
flowers. Produce from north of Kyoto is
used in superbly eclectic creations like
grapes and grilled aubergine marinated
in balsamic, accompanied by bio wines.
49 Saiinsanzo-cho, Ukyo-ku,
T 075 950 0081, www.makerkyoto.com

Toraya Karyo

The most famous name in Japanese sweets is Toraya. The company has been making exquisite *wagashi* (Japanese candy) for half a millennium and you'll find their products at the centre of many a tea ceremony. Try them in Hiroshi Naito's stunning tea room, next door to the former Imperial Palace. It features Japanese cedar, traditional roof tiles and windows affording a lovely rear-garden view. In winter, try the *oshiruko* (a sweet soup of simmering adzuki beans and wasanbon sugar); in summer, cool down with the *ujikintoki kakigori* (shaved ice with matcha syrup and bean paste). The designs of the *namagashi* (fresh confectionery) are changed every fortnight to ensure that they express the season in form and flavour.
400 Hirohashidono-cho, Ichijo-dori,
Karasuma nishi-iru, Kamigyo-ku,
T 075 441 3113, www.toraya-group.co.jp

Awomb

From its beginnings as a pristine, minimal northern Kyoto restaurant, Awomb moved to the city centre, and chef Hiroshi Ujita applied a similar aesthetic to this 80-year-old house, but retained original elements, such as the cypress beams on the top level (above). Crisp white walls meld with bare stone, and the ground floor has a view of an exquisite Japanese garden. The food is equal to its polished setting, and Ujita has conceived a quality DIY sushi experience. Each of the components, from sashimi to seasonings, are artfully presented on a slab of black slate, accompanied by rice, nori sheets and a bamboo roller. When building your own *teori-zushi*, Ujita says the best approach is not to overthink it. Note that last orders are early, at 8pm.
189 Ubayanagi-cho, T 075 204 5543, www.awomb.com

Erutan Restaurant/Bar

Good Nature Station is an eco-conscious hotel and retail hub for natural and organic food, cosmetics and craft that launched in 2019. Headlining its six eateries, Erutan's menu is overseen by Yoji Tokuyoshi, whose restaurant in Milan has a Michelin star, and its Italian-inspired vegetable-centric dishes are imaginatively presented, perhaps with edible flowers. The truffle egg sandwich is a signature starter, while the pasta course might feature deer and berry ragù. Food 'waste' is either inventively reused (panna cotta is made with roasted potato skin, and jam from vegetable and fruit offcuts) or composted and sent back to farmers. The bar offers artisan beer, local Kawaramachi gin, Japanese whisky and green tea.

Good Nature Station, 318-6 Inari-cho,
T 075 352 3714,
goodnaturestation.com

Tan

One of very few restaurants in Kyoto open for breakfast and lunch as well as dinner, Tan is alone in its format of serving large communal plates of home-style cuisine that are passed between amiable diners around one bubinga-wood table. Expect generous servings of seasonal dishes that feature mainly organic ingredients, such as steamed aubergines and burdock root, sake lees soup, and yams, smoked *daikon* (radish) and oyster mushrooms in a cream cheese, sesame and tofu sauce. Launched in 2016 by Yuko Kuwamura, who owns the Michelin-starred Wakuden restaurants, it is located by a canal in a former residence reworked by architect Toshihito Yokouchi. After eating, retire to the upstairs living room for tea as you gaze over the water. *106-13 Gogen-cho, T 075 533 7744, www.tan.kyoto.jp*

Savory

The fruit and vegetable merchants behind this restaurant wanted city-dwellers to see the provenance first hand, so they brought 200 tonnes of soil from their farm in the Tanba region and built a 300 sq m organic plot on a rooftop next to the dining room, which is laid out around it in an L-shape, with floor-to-ceiling windows. There are also beehives and a hydroponic room. A lack of signs indicating what is growing is a ploy to encourage engagement with the on-site farmer. The head chef hails from top Kobe restaurant Comme Chinois, and he turns out creative modern French fare with Japanese inflections in dishes such as vegetable parfait, and steamed aubergine and Iberian pork with smoked corn sauce. *3F, Kyoto Yaoichi Honkan, Higashinotoin-dori, Sanjo-sagaru, T 075 223 2320, www.kyotoyaoichihonkan.com*

Kitcho

Kunio Tokuoka is one of the country's most famous chefs. He's the grandson of Teiichi Yuki, the founder of the Kitcho group – a culinary institution in Japan – and he has taken the flagship to new heights. Using the finest seafood and seasonal vegetables, Tokuoka creates small works of art, served on fine crockery, some of which dates back 400 years. The *kaiseki* meal is served over a three-hour period, so your reservation will be for around 7pm. Diners are seated on low chairs at black lacquer tables in seven discrete private rooms; the five on the ground floor have a view of the garden. An online booking system means you no longer need a concierge with connections to secure a spot, although you will still have to book many months in advance.
58 Susukinobaba-cho, Saga Tenryuji, T 075 881 1101, www.kyoto-kitcho.com

Metro

Every musician who passes through Kyoto seems to play at this basement institution. Owner Nick Yamamoto had a much-loved reggae bar before setting up his club in an underground passage that links to Jingu-Marutamachi station, hence the moniker. Metro started out in 1990 during Japan's garish disco era, and it has hosted acts as disparate as Ben Watt and Thee Michelle Gun Elephant. The longest-running night is Diamonds are Forever, a drag-queen party that launched the same year as the venue did. Increasingly it has also become an arts hub, and teams up with festivals such as Kyotographie to stage events. The space is about as chic as a clapped-out Toyota, but you are guaranteed a memorable time.
Basement, Ebisu Building, 82 Simodutsumi-cho, Kawabata-dori, Marutamachi-sagaru, T 075 752 4765, www.metro.ne.jp

Walden Woods

Fashion and interior designer Seiichiro Shimamura not only pushed the boat out at the completely whitewashed Walden Woods, he pushed the chairs and tables out too. The only seating is on wooden bleachers upstairs, which are set around the sides of the room facing a single tree in the centre. The name and concept were inspired by the US philosopher Henry David Thoreau, who removed himself from society and holed up in a cabin in the woods to reflect on nature before writing *Walden* in 1854. Beans are single origin, the house blend is served pour-over, the chai latte has a kick and, for a local flavour, the matcha is supplied by the famed Rishouen farm. There may be little to eat, but the *canelé* is a winner.
508-1 Sakae-machi, Shimogyu-ku,
T 075 344 9009, www.walden-woods.com

Café Malda

Architect Nobuyuki Fujimoto's three-room hotel/café is filled with the late Japan-based German designer Jurgen Lehl's Babaghuri-brand furniture and textiles (its flagship is over the road). Malda's striking wooden-slat facade complements the organic forms of Lehl's teak stools and tables, pendant lamps and ceramics in the café, while the richly coloured suites feature his bedspreads and other items. The collaboration extends to a sustainable lifestyle. The all-day set meal, always an aromatic veggie curry of local seasonal ingredients with organic rice, a side and raita yoghurt, is based on the fare served at Lehl's canteen, as are its gluten-free muffins. The sudachi citrus and sansho pepper 'salty' gin soda is another treat. *684 Marukizaimoku-cho, Sakaimachi-dori, Nakagyo-ku, T 075 606 5385, www.maldakyoto.com*

Kaboku Tearoom

The origins of the legendary tea supplier Ippodo go back to 1717, but it wasn't until 1846 that its name, meaning 'Preserve the Standard', was coined by Prince Akira Yamashina, in the hope that the company would always provide the nation with its high-quality product, grown near Kyoto in the Uji region. In 1995, Ippodo set up the Kaboku Tearoom adjacent to its main store, which purveys more than 40 types of leaf, from gyokuro to bancha. It is a hands-on experience, where staff supervise as you make your own brew following traditional methods. If you visit in late May or early June, sample the shincha sencha, which is offered straight after picking and prepared as soon as possible, to taste the flavour that left a prince hankering for more.
52 Tokiwagi-cho, Teramachi-dori,
T 075 211 4018, www.ippodo-tea.co.jp

INSIDERS' GUIDE

SARA AIKO AND TAKUMA INOUE, CREATIVE DIRECTORS

Married couple Sara Aiko, founder of Curated Kyoto, and Takuma Inoue, an interior designer who runs hip cultural space Y Gion (19 Benzaiten-cho, T 075 533 8555) are effusive about their city: 'It is built on creativity, spirituality, tradition, innovation and harmony: with others, the surroundings and the seasons. You don't need to visit a tourist site to feel its essence.' Inoue's favourite spot is Kawai Kanjiro's House (569 Kanei-cho, Gojozaka, Higashiyama-ku, T 075 561 3585), where the *mingei* (folk art) potter lived until 1966.

Between culture, he suggests pit stops at sweets café Umezono (180 Fudocho, T 075 241 0577) – 'I grew up with its *mitarashi dango* (rice dumplings)' – and Sour (607-19 Uradera-cho, T 075 231 0778): 'The originator of fresh fruit and veg with *chu-hai* (sweet alcoholic canned drinks)'. Aiko adds: 'Hands down, Yugen (266-2 Daikoku-cho, T 075 606 5062) makes the best green-tea lattes.' At lunch, she is a fan of Kousagisha (113 Kamibaba-cho, Jodoji, T 075 761 7707), an intimate vegan eatery above a gallery. And by night, she 'enjoys the vibe' at Node Hotel art bar (see p023). Inoue loves the Okinawa/Asian fusion cuisine at Berangkat (334 Maruya-cho, Gokomachi-dori, Sanjo-agaru, T 075 255 6667), but they advise: 'Even street ramen is delicious as locals really take pride in the food that they serve.' To escape, they might drive 90 minutes south-west to Awajishima: 'The island has Tadao Ando architecture and great sushi.'
For full addresses, see Resources.

ART AND DESIGN
GALLERIES, STUDIOS AND PUBLIC SPACES

Kyoto's millennium as the cultural capital of Japan has left it with an embarrassment of riches, and you're more likely to find a Kano school masterpiece on a temple wall than behind museum glass. It still produces more than its fair share of artists – Yayoi Kusama, photographer Yasumasa Morimura and sculptor Etsuro Sotoo all studied here. When MoMAK (see p068) opened in 1963, it catalysed an independent scene in Okazaki – Imura (opposite) is the city's top commercial enterprise – and a 2020 wing for contemporary art at Kyocera (see p036) cemented the area's reputation. Elsewhere, seek out Gallery 9.5 at Hotel Anteroom (see p026), En Arts (Gion Kitagawa, T 075 525 2355) near Yasaka-jinja, the university's @KCUA (238-1 Oshiaburanokoji-cho, T 075 253 1509) and the storied Galerie 16 (opposite), which, since 1962, has shown many of the country's leading lights from Shigeyoshi Iwata to Morimura, Kodai Nakahara and Kosugi+Ando. Kyoto International Manga Museum (Karasuma-dori, T 075 254 7414) celebrates arguably Japan's most successful artform; the wartime mangas-with-a-message are fascinating.

Over the past decade, a coterie of young craftsmen at the helm of historic firms has revitalised traditional techniques, typified by Hosoo (see p066). Other heritage firms, such as Kaikado (see p095) simply continue to produce superb timeless pieces. For avant-garde ceramics, head to Sokyo (381-2 Motomachi, T 075 746 4456). *For full addresses, see Resources.*

Imura Art Gallery

Yuzo Imura's commercial gallery, set in a striking white box in the arts district, is a little space with a huge reputation. Since launching in 1990, Imura has shown an eye for local talent: 'I look for artists who connect the traditional and contemporary to try to create something new from Kyoto.' His growing roster includes Masaomi Raku, who sculpts sensual abstract shapes from granite; lacquer master Satoshi Someya, who uses horns, bones and twigs in cheeky takes on Japanese icons, from tea bowls to deer heads; photographer Yoshihiro Tatsuki ('Blowing in the Left Hand Wind', above); and ceramic artist Takashi Hinoda. Nearby, also check out the museums (see p036), Mori Yu (see p069), and Galerie 16 (T 075 751 9238), just to the south in Gion. *31 Kawabata-higashi, Marutamachi, T 075 761 7372, www.imuraart.com*

House of Hosoo

A shining example of how to keep artisanry relevant, Hosoo was founded in 1688 and made its name weaving kimono belts, but 12th-generation master Masataka Hosoo changed direction and invested in larger looms to produce fabric for fashion labels like Chanel and D or. Now he has Masaya Kushino requesting material for shoes for Lady Gaga. The effect is rippling through the Nishijin district where each production step is executed by a different craftsman. Opened in 2019, the design of its flagship is based on traditional building methods, with layered walls of compacted local clay, and black-ink plaster and gold trim on the facade. As well as material, it offers lifestyle items such as bags, slippers and cushions; upstairs (above) hosts textile exhibitions.
412 Kakimoto-cho, T 075 441 5189,
www.hosoo-kyoto.com

National Museum of Modern Art

The permanent collection at the museum, known locally as MoMAK, includes art from the East and West. Duchamp's fountain shares the limelight with *nihonga* painting, a style that dates to the 1860s – seek out work by modern masters Kagaku Murakami and Shoen Uemura – and contemporary Japanese photography including Kyoichi Tsuzuki's 'Happy Victims' series. The 1986 building, designed by Fumihiko Maki, is low key, considering its five storeys and nearly 10,000 sq m of floor space. The steel-grid facade gives it the heft to stand up to the next-door ROHM Theatre (see p035); glass pillars supply the sensitivity it needs in a picturesque park. Enter via a cavernous lobby and climb the staircase to the winding corridors of the gallery.
26-1 Okazaki Enshoji-cho, T 075 761 4111, www.momak.go.jp

Mori Yu Gallery

Since 2001, in a revamped townhouse with a serene black facade, whitewashed ceiling beams and splotches on the floor, Mori Yu has been supporting emerging talent from the region who show an understanding of Japanese tradition, in particular the Rinpa school and the craftsmanship of the Edo and Meiji eras. Exhibition highlights have included Manavu Muragishi's pop-culture bricolages; Masayuki Kawai's lo-tech video art, in which cables and circuit boards are part of the piece; and Hiroshi Fuji's large-scale cartoony dinosaur installations built up from discarded Happy Meal and other plastic toys – an arresting statement on waste in today's consumer society. Group show 'Undulationism VII' included paintings by local heavyweight Aki Kuroda (above).
4-19 Rengezo-cho, Shogoin,
T 075 950 5230, www.moriyu-gallery.com

Tofukuji gardens

Japanese landscaping is an artform in itself. The pre-eminent exponents were Muso Soseki (1275-1351), whose Saihoji (T 075 391 3631) is moss heaven; Kobori Enshu (1579-1647), who laid out Sento Gosho (T 075 211 1215) in the Imperial Palace grounds; and Mirei Shigemori, who created the gardens at Tofukuji in 1939. Do not miss this delightful 1236 Zen complex en route to the torii-fest at Fushimi Inari (T 075 641 7331). Four distinct environments surround the head priest's quarters. The dry South Garden (above) is the most traditional; the rocks symbolise the Elysian Fields. Elsewhere, a patchwork of shrubs and gravel merges into another area in which small stone squares dot a carpet of moss.

778-15 Hon-machi, Higashiyama-ku, T 075 561 0087, www.tofukuji.jp

ARCHITOUR

A GUIDE TO KYOTO'S ICONIC BUILDINGS

This is a historical treasure trove, boasting more than 4,800 shrines and temples, dating back over a thousand years. German architect Bruno Taut paid a visit to the 17th-century Katsura Rikyu Imperial Villa (Katsura Misono, Nishikyo-ku, sankan.kunaicho.go.jp) in 1933 and hailed it as a pre-modernist masterpiece; later Le Corbusier and Gropius made pilgrimages. Entry is restricted – apply online, well in advance. For relatively contemporary Japanese landscaping, head to the various gardens in the Tofukuji temple complex (see p070), a tour de force by the feted designer Mirei Shigemori.

Kyoto does not simply live off its past, however, and since the 1990s there have been a number of impressive additions. Among these are Arata Isozaki's dark terracotta-clad Kyoto Concert Hall (1-26 Shimogamo Hangi-cho, Sakyo-ku, T 075 711 2980); Shin Takamatsu's intervention at Higashi Honganji (see p077); Tadao Ando's boat-like riverside retail complexes Times I and II (Sanjo Kiyamachi); Fumio Toki's Kansai-kan of the National Diet Library (8-1-3 Seikadai, Seika-cho, Soraku-gun, T 077 498 1200), with its 250m granite waterfall, 35km south of the city; and Hiroshi Hara's 1997 central station (see p010). Wary of opposition to his futurist design, Hara laid it out according to Kyoto's 1,200-year-old grid, ensuring it did not cast any shadow on surrounding buildings. Most doubters were won over, and it provides a most fitting welcome. *For full addresses, see Resources.*

Daigoji Gojunoto

Erected in 951, the 38m-tall, five-storey pagoda of the Daigoji temple, located just south of the city, is Kyoto's oldest structure (much of the ancient capital was destroyed during the 15th-century Onin War), and an official national treasure. Constructed when Japanese Shingon Buddhism was still developing, the building retains the classic formality of a shrine on the exterior, while the walls and ceiling of the ground floor inside are adorned with a series of striking mandalas. The surrounding *kaiyushiki-teien* (stroll garden) is highly unusual, combining the *chisen-teien* style (featuring a pond) and a *karesansui-teien* (dry rock) section, consisting of carefully placed stones and raked pebbles. The best way to view the garden is to take a walk around the water. *22 Higashi Oji-cho, Daigo, Fushimi-ku, T 075 571 0002, www.daigoji.or.jp*

International Conference Centre

Legendary architect Sachio Otani designed this trapezoid neo-brutalist building, which announced its presence below Mount Hiei in 1966. Best known as the venue where the Kyoto Protocol on climate change was agreed, it served as a set for 1974 film *The Yakuza*. There are now four huge congress halls (Annex, opposite). The main one has a capacity of 1,840 underneath a massive disc-shaped reflective plate, also devised by Otani, that symbolises the sky, with spotlights giving the impression of stars. Furniture by midcentury modernist Isamu Kenmochi is employed throughout, and the 'Anraku Isu' chairs in the lobby were created especially for the complex. Stroll around the concrete paths by the lake or book in advance for a free monthly tour.
Takaragaike, Sakyo-ku, T 075 705 1218,
www.icckyoto.or.jp

Face House

Architect Kazumasa Yamashita's creation seems to openly laugh at convention, and its anthropomorphic facade has enchanted passers-by for decades. It is as functional as it is weird. The 'mouth' is a French-door entrance, the 'eyes' are bedroom windows and the left 'ear' comprises two verandahs. Only the 'nose' might be called superfluous, although it does allow a shaft of light inside. Built in 1974, when architecture in Japan was at its most experimental, the humorous design is simply uncategorisable. It could be argued either that it defied the trends of minimalism, brutalism, metabolism and postmodernism or that it put a 'face' to all of them combined. On the ground floor, Ooo (T 075 203 9259) is a welcoming and aptly offbeat studio/store brimming with cute miscellaneous goods in a rainbow of hues. *740-1 Tatedaionji-cho, Nakagyo-ku*

Higashi Honganji Reception Hall

The monks responsible for looking after this 1602 temple made a surprisingly bold choice when they picked Shin Takamatsu, known for his abstract, sci-fi structures, to create a new auditorium. Yet Takamatsu indulged his flair for the dramatic without disrupting the ancient environs by placing everything out of sight. Apart from a small entrance, from ground level all you see is a crescent and circle skylight, straight out of his space-age style book, which glow at night. A corridor gallery lined with relics leads to the centrepiece: a great concrete cone that envelops a 300-seat seminar room. Look right as you enter the complex to see Goichi Takeda's 1934 reception hall, built in a far more conservative era. *Karasuma-dori, Shichijo-agaru, Shimogyo-ku, T 075 371 9181, www.higashihonganji.or.jp*

Issey Miyake

Kyoto's *machiya* renaissance includes some outstanding renovations but few reach the level of conceptual coherency here. Naoto Fukasawa suffused his vision, completed in 2018, with shades of *sumi* (charcoal). He restored the 134-year-old facade, returning it to its original appearance, and its clay roof tiles, latticed wood facade and ramie *noren* are a celebration of another era. Inside, a mezzanine and mottled concrete floors complement the timber beams, all a perfect foil for Issey Miyake's colourful brands. The highlight is in the courtyard. Set in a sea of pebbles, a standalone *kura* (storehouse) is now an exhibition space. A past presentation on Ikko Tanaka's seminal 1990 show 'Graphic Art Botanical Garden' provided the back story to the designer's prints on IM garments and accessories.
89 Tsuchiya-cho, Sanjo-sagaru, Yanaginobanba-dori, T 075 254 7540, www.isseymiyake.com

SHOPS

THE BEST RETAIL THERAPY AND WHAT TO BUY

Centuries-old artisan studios and manufacturers abound in Kyoto. Pick up handmade knives and kitchen utensils from Aritsugu (219 Kajiya-cho, Nishikikoji-dori, T 075 221 1091), a *sensu* folding fan at Miyawaki Baisenan (80-3 Daikoku-cho, Rokkaku-dori, Tominokoji Higashi-iru, T 075 221 0181) and *senko* incense sticks, with aromas from *yuzu* citrus to cherry blossom, at Kungyokudo (101 Sakai-cho, Horikawa-dori, Shimogyo-ku, T 075 371 0162), or the contemporary brand Lisn (Cocon Karasuma, 620 Suiginya-cho, T 075 353 6468), which has a vast range presented on undulating glass shelves. For more craft interpretations, Kohchosai Kosuga (74 Nakajima-cho, Sanjo-dori, T 075 221 8687) specialises in bamboo, and Tohgoro (539-6 Gojobashi-higashi, T 075 561 0056) modernises Kyo-ware ceramics, while paper and print specialist Ko Kado of Kamisoe (11-1 Fujinomori-cho, Murasakino-higashi, Kita-ku, T 075 432 8555) is just one of a promising new wave of makers putting a spin on heritage.

Retail is not solely about the traditional. Katsuji Wakisaka's wildly popular cluster of Sou Sou stores (583-3 Nakano-cho, Shinkyogoku-dori, T 075 212 8005) offer bright, gaudy phone cases and split-toe sneakers, and there's directional fashion at Lloomm (see p083) and Rainmaker (see p088), and homewares and furniture at Songbird (see p090) and Sfera (see p094). If your purchase is a gift (or even if not), say *purezento desu*, and it will be beautifully wrapped for free. *For full addresses, see Resources.*

Kotoshina

Reviving a long-neglected ancient beauty secret – the moisturising benefits of green-tea-seed oil – Kotoshina collaborates with a plantation in the Uji region to create its organic skincare range, which is blended with Gamarde-les-Bains spring water and fragranced by a historic French perfumer. Its headline 'Beauty Oil' is 70 per cent green-tea-seed oil with the rest evening primrose, African baobab, argan, rice germ and camellia seed oils. In this concession on the ground floor of the Bal department store, servers in crisp white lab coats extol the virtues of more than 20 other cosmetics made from green-tea extracts. Kotoshina products are used in spa treatments at the Four Seasons (see p030) and sold there too.
Bal, 251 Yamazaki-cho, Kawaramachi-dori, Sanjo-sagaru, T 075 223 0503, www.kotoshina-kyoto.com

D&Department

For this incarnation of Kenmei Nagaoka's project to showcase craftsmanship from every nook of the prefecture (and the rest of Japan), he collaborated with students at the Kyoto University of Art and Design, who help source products, and the monks of a 13th-century temple, who provided the real estate. Neat tags on each item reveal its provenance and when it was produced, and nothing is put on sale unless a long lifespan is guaranteed. We bought a 'Rug From Lifestock' (above, ¥5,500) made from layered wool samples produced in Aichi and Gifu prefectures. Across the gravel yard is a café, where low chairs by Tendo Mokkou are a counterpoint to the mini Buddhist altar. Light meals use seasonal ingredients from growers who share Nagaoka's ethos. *397 Shinkai-cho, T 075 343 3217, www.d-department.com*

Lloomm

A *noren* and a small nameplate on a quiet residential street are all that indicate the entrance to this hidden-away streetwear store, enhancing its hip, exclusive vibe. Down a narrow alley, in a tiny landscaped garden, Lloomm occupies a former *kura* (storehouse) converted by Ninkipen!, who inserted French doors and a mezzanine, and interiors of unvarnished timber that emit a woody aroma. The spotlighting is by Nara firm New Light Pottery. On the rails is a line-up of urban brands, mostly unisex and oversized clothing, including Japanese labels Archon, Gourmet Jeans, Midorikawa, Marvine Pontiak and Unused. Also on sale are casual men's shoes by Foot the Coacher and Hender Scheme's leather accessories. *224-1 Nabeya-cho, Takatsuji-agaru, Fuyacho-dori, Shimogyo-ku, T 075 354 0373, www.lloomm.jp*

Uchu Wagashi
Even for minimalist-leaning Kyoto, this confectionery shop is bare. Its speciality is *higashi* (long-lasting 'dry' sweets) made from wasanbon sugar that's refined for 20 days before it is coloured, flavoured and pressed into wood moulds. Shapes classically resemble flowers or seasonal motifs but Uchu's playful designs include aeroplanes, penguins and pigs' snouts.
307 Shintomi-cho, T 075 754 8538

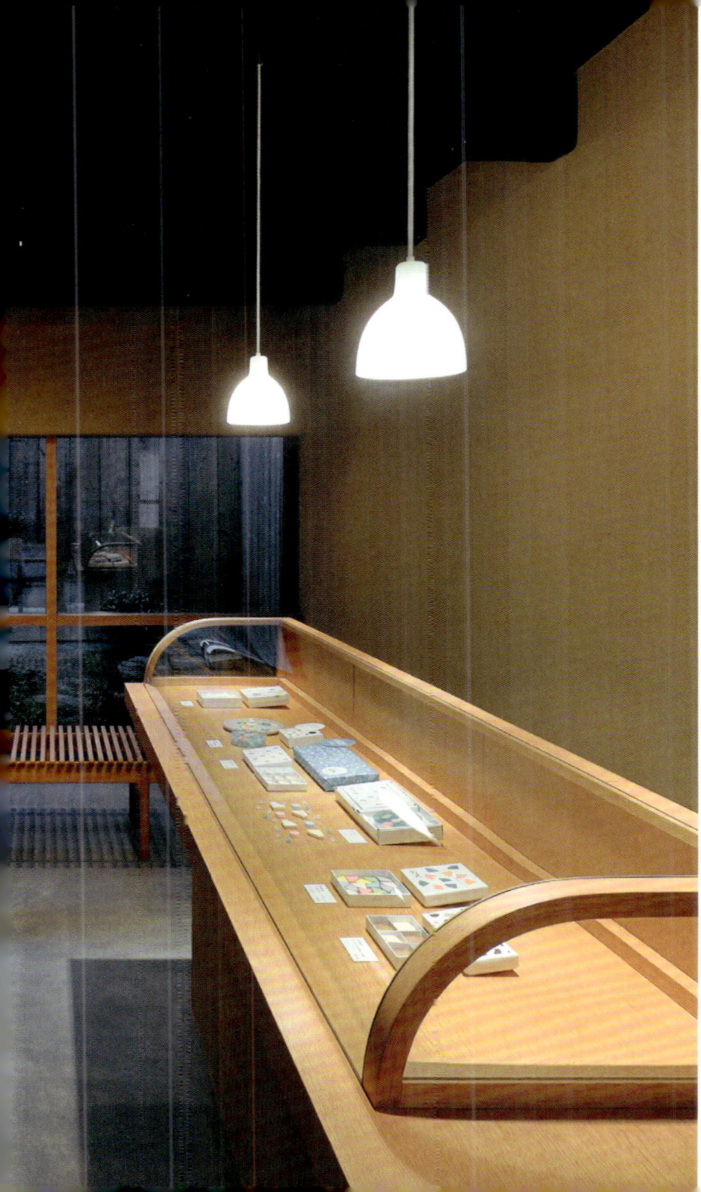

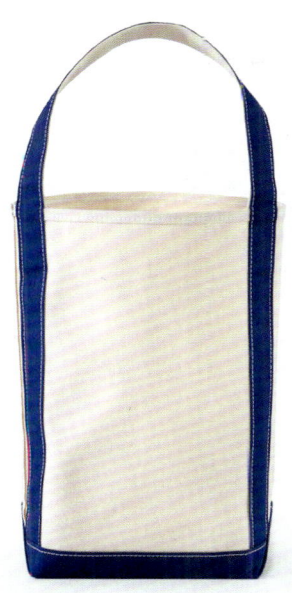

Tembea

Japanese brand Tembea is renowned for its high-quality heavy-duty canvas bags. They are made from combed cotton-fibre yarn treated with paraffin wax to waterproof it and woven on a 50-year-old shuttle loom, giving rise to a lustrous appearance and selvedge that is celebrated in the design. From the deep and tall 'Baguette' (above, ¥11,550), the first model off the production line, names have referenced inspirations and uses. Landscape Products' pared-back interior features raw concrete floors, box shelving and custom-made wooden tables, and seasonal colourways hang on a single rail running along one wall. The majority of the range is totes, but there are also a few other styles, as well as leather wallets.

527 Hoteiya-cho, Fuyacho-higashi-iru, Ebisugawa-dori, Nakagyo-ku, T 075 221 5278, www.torso-design.com

Rainmaker

Koichi Watanabe initially teamed up with Ryutaro Kishi in 2008 to launch N4, before the duo established Rainmaker in 2012. Watanabe says the brand vision aligns with a Gustav Mahler quote: 'Tradition is not the worship of ashes, but the preservation of fire.' In practice, that means classically cut menswear with bold twists. Cardigans come with kimono collars, bomber jackets are embroidered with Japanese motifs, and denim outerwear has knitted sleeves. A range of tailored jackets constitutes the centrepiece of each collection, but the pair design everything from tasselled loafers to paper hats. They work from a studio beneath the store – a minimalist concrete and glass affair – producing both ready-to-wear and made-to-measure items. *502 Eboshiya-cho, T 075 708 2280, www.rainmaker-kyoto.com*

Songbird Design Store

Husband-and-wife Masaki and Akiko Tokuda's café/design store occupies a minimalist, concrete-floored former inn. You may have to ask them to open up the shop (above). Masaki's work has a playful feel (so Kyoto), from the 'Incense House Set', with sticks set in chimneys, to the 'Bird House Clock' and the 'Moss' rug in the shape of a big splodge. In the second-floor café, you can try out the 'Songbird Chair Arm' – like his other furniture, it's very boxy. On the menu is an egg curry plated to resemble a bird's nest and an excellent take on the omelette sandwich, a peculiar local culinary obsession. If you like the bulbous mugs, buy them on the way out, along with totes and stationery. Note the hours: last orders are at 7pm.
529 Nishi Takeya-machi, Nakagyo-ku, T 075 252 2781, www.songbird-design.jp

Uragu

The name of this stationery store, opened in 2006, means both 'joyful' and 'tool that discreetly assists people', which is apt for the products – paper, letter-writing sets, postcards and envelopes featuring designs by graphic art firm Goodman, headed by Yoshiyuki Ohno. Situated at the far end of a narrow Gion alley, Uragu is also one of Kyoto's most secreted-away shops – do not even attempt to find it without a map.

Behind the *noren* curtains and wooden door, walls are painted a stunning *asagi* green-blue. Look out for the best-selling 'Mameno', ¥410, a traditional memo pad. In the humid summer months, you will no doubt desire a hand-printed folding fan made by Nishino Kobo, a local company that has been crafting them since 1912.
4-297 Miyagawa-suji, T 075 551 1357, www.uragu.com

Otsuka Gofukuten
Kimono merchant Otsuka Gofukuten
opened this stylish flagship in a former
tofu shop, overhauled by Yusuke Seki,
who installed oak shelving and carved
new textures into the existing tiles. The
designs are modern: you're more likely
to find neon houndstooth than cherry
blossom. Invest in a pure cotton version.
88-1 Hoshino-cho, Higashiyama-ku,
T 075 533 0533, www.otsuka-gofukuten.jp

Sfera Shop

Spread across the five floors of the Sfera Building are a bookshop selling design, architecture, food and art titles; a café; a bar; and a gallery. And housed on the first level, the Sfera Shop (above) purveys the often pared-down art and craft offerings of Japanese designers like Shuji Nakagawa (utensils made from sawara cypress) and Shigeru Teraji (metal sake jugs and pans), as well as global names, such as Edward Wohl. We picked up a set of corrugated oak candleholders detailed with semaphore-like slices of brass and copper, conceived by the brand's creative director Shigeo Mashiro. The Sfera Building itself, the work of Claesson Koivisto Rune, is cloaked in a titanium facade perforated with a cherry-blossom-leaf pattern by Markus Moström. *1F, 17 Benzaiten-cho, T 075 532 1105, www.ricordi-sfera.com*

Kaikado

Founded here in 1875, Kaikado pioneered the crafting of *chazutsu* (tea caddies) in the early Meiji era, replacing earthenware jars. The airtight cylindrical design, unchanged for more than a century, is handmade using up to 130 processes and features an inner layer of tin and an outer layer of tin, brass or copper that develops a patina over time. Ideal for storing tea leaves, coffee beans, herbs and spices, the entire range (water pitcher, above, ¥55,000) is on display at the Shimogyo-ku flagship (T 075 351 5788) but we highly recommend seeking out the hip Kaikado Café (T 075 353 5668) nearby, which also carries a covetable selection. Set in a tram depot revamped by Danish firm Oeo Studio, it has concrete walls, oak furniture by Another Country and copper light fixtures that complement the wares. *www.kaikado.jp*

ESCAPES

WHERE TO GO IF YOU WANT TO LEAVE TOWN

Kyoto is the perfect base from which to explore Japan. It is just a short train journey to the bright lights of Osaka, for great street eats and a much wilder nightlife; or to the picturesque ancient capital of Nara (see p100), which feels like a quaint town, albeit one dotted with huge 8th-century temples; or to cosmopolitan Kobe. The port was badly hit by the 1995 earthquake but a contemporary city has risen from the rubble. It also has some of the best beef on the planet.

If you've more time on your hands, it's three hours by train and ferry to Naoshima in the Seto Inland Sea, where you are greeted by a Yayoi Kusama pumpkin sitting on the end of the pier, and Tadao Ando has created three museums for the extraordinary Benesse Art Site – Chichu (3449-1 Naoshima, T 087 892 3755), Lee Ufan (1390 Azakuraura) and Minamidera (Honmura, T 087 892 3223), which has a light installation by James Turrell. The trail now extends to the nearby islands of Teshima and Inujima, which have art spaces designed by Ryue Nishizawa and Hiroshi Sambuichi respectively.

Alternatively, you could head two hours east to Gifu to visit the bonkers Site of Reversible Destiny (1298-2 Takabayashi, Yoro-cho, Yoro-gun, T 058 432 0501) – a park with nine surreal buildings dreamt up by the late New York poet Madeline Gins and Nagoya artist Shusaku Arakawa – and on to the outstanding contemporary gallery (opposite) in the otherwise traditional city of Kanazawa. *For full addresses, see Resources.*

Contemporary Art Museum, Kanazawa

The 21st Century Museum of Contemporary Art, to give it its full name, is reason alone to make the two-hour 10-minute train trip to Kanazawa. Designed by SANAA, it has a circular glass facade encasing a jumble of box-like spaces of various sizes, enabling free circulation through the building. Art is also installed in the surrounding park. The collection has many unexpected delights, such as Argentine Leandro Erlich's optical illusion *The Swimming Pool* and Belgian Jan Fabre's cleverly placed sculpture *The Man Who Measures The Clouds*. Known as Little Kyoto, Kanazawa has fewer temples, but the old samurai stronghold Ninjadera (T 076 241 0888), full of tunnels, trapdoors and false stairs, and the Kenrokuen garden (T 076 234 3800) are well worth visiting. *1-2-1 Hirosaka, T 076 220 2800, www.kanazawa21.jp*

Setouchi Aonagi, Matsuyama

This seven-room retreat outside the city of Matsuyama is an exquisite Tadao Ando work perched 450m up in the hills. Built in 1998 as a guesthouse, it was also run as a small art museum before reopening in this guise. Ando oversaw each transformation, and his minimalist signature manifests itself in swathes of bare concrete, straight lines and a neutral palette. Book the duplex Aonagi Suite (above) for its huge windows and terrace with views of the Seto Inland Sea. Other highlights here are a lap pool (opposite) that seems to extend into the horizon and the *kaiseki* dinners. Nearby is one of Japan's oldest hot springs, Dogo Onsen (⌐ 089 921 5141), and its Meiji-era bathhouse. Matsuyama city is four hours by train from Kyoto, changing at Okayama. *794-1 Yanaidani-cho, T 089 977 9500, www.setouchi-aonagi.com*

Noborioji Hotel, Nara

Behind an unassuming facade, Noborioji has a sumptuous interior characterised by rich wood panelling, while the expansive windows celebrate its lush surroundings. A bijou hotel, its 14 rooms are conversely large by Japanese standards, restaurant Le Bois serves French cuisine with a twist, and there's a classy whisky bar as well as a gym. Less than an hour by train south of Kyoto, Nara was Japan's first permanent capital, from 710 to 784, and its ancient Buddhist temples and Shinto shrines are still standing. The most impressive is the 8th-century Todaiji, which remains one of the largest wooden structures in the world, despite being rebuilt twice (due to fire), and on a smaller scale. It nestles in Nara Park, where 1,200 deer roam free. *40-1 Noborioji-cho, T 012 099 5546, www.noborioji.com*

Byodoin Museum, Uji

The profile of Japan's almost 1,000-year-old temple Byodoin is so iconic that its Phoenix Hall was chosen to grace the ¥10 coin. Surrounded by a *jodo-shiki* (paradise-type) garden and built in part over a pond, it appears to float. Architect Akira Kuryu was entrusted with adding a museum to the site. He created an abstract representation of Phoenix Hall executed in glass, steel and textured concrete that stands in complete harmony with the landscape. It houses various national treasures, including 26 statues of Unchu Kuyo Bosatsu and the original temple bell. It is located 20km south of Kyoto, in Uji. Across the river is the 11th-century Ujigami-jinja (T 077 421 4634), the oldest shrine in the country, with its distinctive asymmetrical roof.
116 Ujirenge, T 077 421 2861,
www.byodoin.or.jp

Miho Museum, Shigaraki
IM Pei has made the most of a forested,
mountainous site an hour from Kyoto.
The approach to this museum of Eastern
and Western antiquities, which is mostly
buried in a hill, is via a tunnel and over a
high bridge. The geometries of the main
atrium (pictured) set the scene. A louvred
glass roof is held up on triangles of steel,
with walls and floors of warm limestone.
300 Tashiro Momodani, T 074 882 3411

NOTES

SKETCHES AND MEMOS

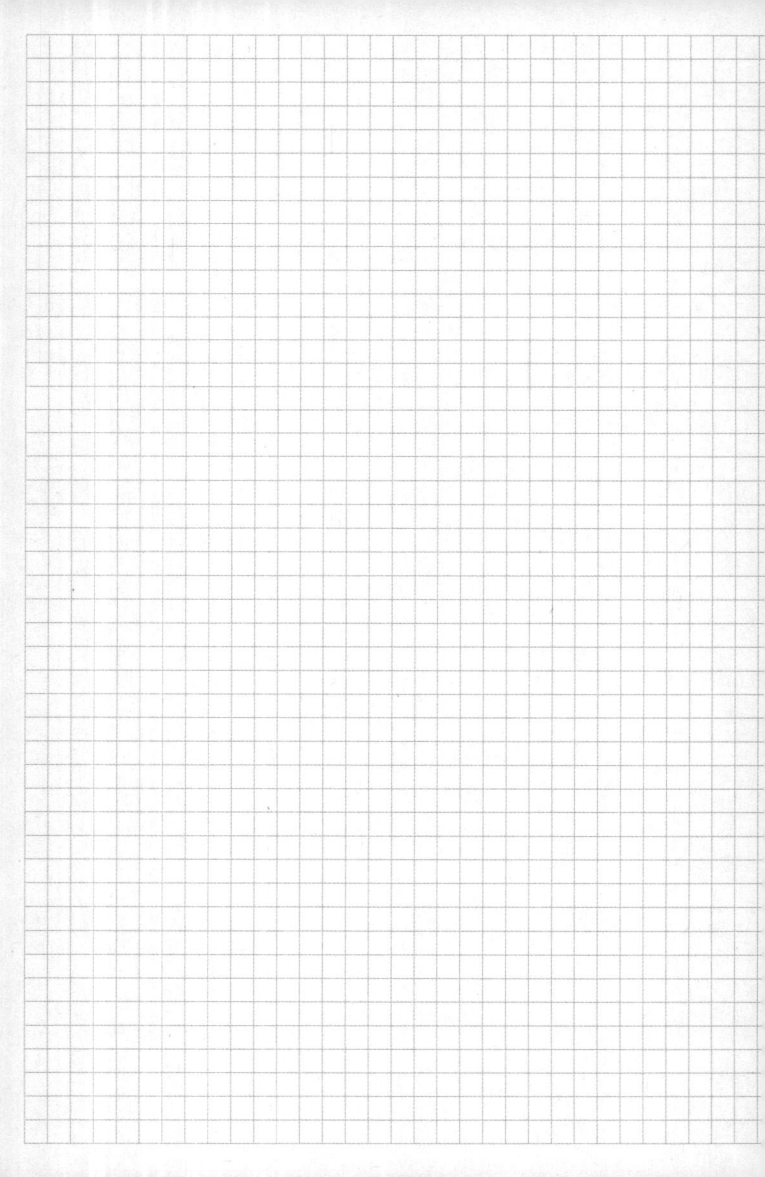

RESOURCES
CITY GUIDE DIRECTORY

A

Aritsugu 080
219 Kajiya-cho
Nishikikoji-dori
T 075 221 1091
www.kyoto-nishiki.or.jp

Awomb 051
189 Ubaynagi-cho
T 075 204 5543
www.awomb.com

B

Bar Rocking Chair 046
434-2 Tachibana-cho
Gokomachi-dori
Bukkoji-sagaru
Shimogyo-ku
T 075 496 8679
www.bar-rockingchair.jp

Berangkat 062
334 Maruya-cho
Gokomachi-dori
Sanjo-agaru
T 075 255 6667

Bungalow 040
15 Kashiwaya-cho
T 075 256 8205
www.bungalow.jc

Byodoin Museum 101
116 Ujirenge
Uji
T 077 421 2861
www.byodoin.or.jp

C

Café Malda 060
684 Marukizaimoku-cho
Sakaimachi-dori
Nakagyo-ku
T 075 606 5385
www.maldakyoto.com

Chichu Art Museum 096
3449-1 Naoshima
Kagawa
T 087 892 3755
www.benesse-artsite.jp

Cinematik Saloon 032
7F
410 Shimomaruya-cho
T 075 251 0995
www.cinematiksaloon.com

D

D&Department 082
397 Shinkai-cho
T 075 343 3215
www.d-department.com

Daigoji Gojunoto 073
22 Higashi Oji-cho
Fushimi-ku
Daigo
T 075 571 0002
www.daigoji.or.jp

Davada Coffee & Records 044
469-11 Zaimoku-cho

Dohjicai Gallery of Art 043
1928 Building
56 Benkeiishi-cho
Sanjo Gokomachi
T 075 256 6155
www.dohjidai.com

E

En Arts 064
Gion Kitagawa
T 075 525 2355
www.en-arts.com

HOTELS

ADDRESSES AND ROOM RATES

Ace 016
Room rates:
double, from ¥35,000
245-2 Kurumaya-cho
T 075 229 9001
www.acehotel.com/kyoto

Hotel Anteroom 026
Room rates:
double, from ¥10,000;
Terrace Twin Room, from ¥15,000
7 Aketa-cho
Higashi-kujo
Minami-ku
T 075 681 5656
hotel-anteroom.com

Bijuu 028
Room rates:
double, from ¥35,000;
Room 301, from ¥50,000;
Room 501, from ¥95,000
194 Sendo-cho
Kiyamachi-dori
Shijo-sagaru
T 075 353 0802
www.bijuu.jp

BnA Alter Museum 024
Room rates:
double, from ¥15,000;
Continuum, prices on request;
Galápagos Danchi, prices on request
267-1 Tenma-cho
Shimogyo-ku
T 075 748 1278
www.bnaaltermuseum.com

Four Seasons 030
Room rates:
double, from ¥95,000;
Premier Garden View, from ¥95,000
445-3 Myohoin Maekawa-cho
T 075 541 8288
www.fourseasons.com/kyoto

The General 031
double, from ¥16,600
241-1 Nabeya-cho
Takatsuji-agaru
Fuyacho-dori
T 075 746 3697
www.globalhotels.jp

Hiiragiya 022
Room rates:
double, from ¥36,000;
Jun Michida extension room, from
¥42,000;
Tokubetsu-shitsu room, from ¥82,000
per person
Nakahakusan-cho
Fuyacho-dori
Aneyakoji-agaru
T 075 221 1136
www.hiiragiya.co.jp

Hoshinoya 027
Room rates:
double, from ¥106,000;
Tsukihashi Villa, prices on request
11-2 Genrokuzan-cho
T 075 871 0001
www.hoshinoya.com/kyoto

Hotel Kanra 017
  Room rates:
  double, from ¥30,000;
  Kanra Suite, from ¥100,000
  190 Kitamachi
  Karasuma-dori
  Rokujo-sagaru
  Shimogyo-ku
  T 075 344 3815
  www.hotelkanra.jp
Kumagusuku 016
  Room rates:
  double, from ¥6,500
  37-3 Mibubamba-cho
  Nakagyo-ku
  T 075 432 8168
  www.kumagusuku.info
Maja 016
  Room rates:
  hut, from ¥5,000
  92 Tsuchiya-cho
  Yanaginobamba-dori
  T 075 205 5477
  www.maja-hotel.com
9h 018
  Room rates:
  pod, from ¥5,300
  588 Teianmaeno-cho
  Teramachi-dori
  Shijo-sagaru
  T 075 353 7337
  www.ninehours.co.jp/kyoto

Noborioji Hotel 100
  Room rates:
  double, from ¥66,000
  40-1 Noborioji-cho
  Nara
  T 012 099 5546
  www.noborioji.com
Node Hotel 023
  Room rates:
  double, from ¥16,000
  461 Toroyama-cho
  T 075 221 8800
  www.nodehotel.com
RC Hotel 019
  Room rates:
  double, from ¥16,000;
  Room 302, from ¥16,000
  370 Yasaka Kamimachi
  Higashiyama-ku
  T 075 354 5406
  www.rchotelkyoto.com
Setouchi Aonagi 098
  Room rates:
  double, from ¥52,000;
  Aonagi Suite, from ¥83,000 per person
  794-1 Yanaidani-cho
  Matsuyama
  T 089 977 9500
  www.setouchi-aonagi.com

Shiki Juraku 023
  Room rates:
  double, from ¥35,000;
  Ichi-go No 1, from ¥40,000
  165 Konoe-cho
  Shimodachiuri-agaru
  Aburanokoji-dori
  Kamigyo-ku
  T 075 417 0210
  www.shikijuraku.com
Sowaka 016
  Room rates:
  double, from ¥42,000
  480 Kiyoi-cho
  Yasaka Toriimae-sagaru
  T 075 541 5323
  www.sowaka.com
22 Pieces 016
  Room rates:
  apartment, from ¥17,800
  9-4 Higashikujo Muromachi
  Minami-ku
  T 075 644 5115
  www.22pieces.jp

WALLPAPER* CITY GUIDES

Executive Editor
Jeremy Case

Authors
JJ O'Donoghue
Mio Yamada

Art Editor
Jade R Arroyo

Editorial Assistant
Josh Lee

Photography Assistant
Freya Anderson

Photography Editor
Rebecca Moldenhauer

Contributors
Matthew Larking
Nicholas Coldicott
Sean McGeady
Daniëlle Siobhán Mol
Emma Kalkhoven

Interns
Alex Merola
Hannah Makonnen

Kyoto Imprint
First published 2008
Fourth edition 2020

ISBN 978 1 83866 112 0

More City Guides
www.phaidon.com/travel

Follow us
@wallpaperguides

Contact
wcg@phaidon.com

Original Design
Loran Stosskopf

Map Illustrator
Russell Bell

Production Controller
Lily Rodgers

Wallpaper* Magazine
161 Marsh Wall
London E14 9AP
contact@wallpaper.com

Wallpaper*® is a
registered trademark
of TI Media

Phaidon Press Limited
Regent's Wharf
All Saints Street
London N1 9PA

Phaidon Press Inc
65 Bleecker Street
New York, NY 10012

All prices and venue
information are correct
at time of going to press,
but are subject to change.

A CIP Catalogue record for
this book is available from
the British Library.

PHOTOGRAPHERS

KYOTO
A COLOUR-CODED GUIDE TO THE HOT 'HOODS

ARASHIYAMA
The mountains, which are crisscrossed by trails, provide a spectacular backdrop to the city

KINKAKUJI
This peaceful district boasts unmissable temples and gardens like the Golden Pavilion

GINKAKUJI
Visit the Ginkakuji shrine and embark on a spiritual journey along the Philosopher's Path

OKAZAKI
Tour the excellent art museums and galleries, and Heianjingu, entered via a giant *torii*

KARASUMA/KAWARAMACHI
Head to the central areas to browse hip boutiques, department stores and design ateliers

GION/HIGASHIYAMA
Bordered by the river, Kyoto's ancient heart is also home to some of its finest restaurants

For a full description of each neighbourhood, see the Introduction.
Featured venues are colour-coded, according to the district in which they are located.